Arctic Foxes

Victoria Blakemore

vblakemore.author@gmail.com

Copyright info/picture credits

Cover, nialat/AdobeStock; Page 3, tpsdave/Pixabay; Page 5, tpsdave/Pixabay; Page 7, nialat/AdobeStock; Page 9, Hunta/Adobestock; Pages 10-11, Gunnar/AdobeStock; Page 13, skeeze/Pixabay; Page 15, mtnmichelle/AdobeStock; Page 17, tpsdave/Pixabay; Page 19, skeeze/Pixabay; Page 21, llagam/Pixabay; Page 23; diapicard/Pixabay; Page 25, diapicard/Pixabay; Page 27, tpsdave/Pixabay; Page 29, tpsdave/Pixabay; Page 31, Pexels/Pixabay; Page 33, tpsdave/Pixabay

Table of Contents

What Are Arctic Foxes?

Arctic foxes are small mammals. They have white fur that changes color to brown each year.

Arctic foxes have many **adaptations** that help them to live in the frozen Arctic tundra.

Arctic foxes can use their

bushy tail to stay warm. They

wrap it around their body like

a scarf. **3**

Arctic foxes are usually between one and three feet long. Their tail adds another foot to their length.

Arctic foxes can weigh anywhere between six and twenty-one pounds.

Male Arctic foxes are

usually larger than female

Arctic foxes.

Arctic foxes have special features to keep them warm. They have a very thick coat of fur and furry soles on the bottom of their paws.

Their short ears do not allow much heat to leave their body.

Arctic foxes have a pointed

snout. It helps them catch

prey in the snow.

Habitat

Arctic foxes are found in the frozen tundra. The land there is usually covered in snow and ice. They do not live close to the **coast**.

During the summer months, they are often seen along the edges of forests.

Arctic foxes are found in the Arctic Circle. It is the area of land and ocean around the North Pole.

They are found in places like Canada, Russia, Iceland, Alaska, Greenland, and Norway.

Diet

Arctic foxes are **omnivores**, which means that they eat meat and plants.

Their diet is made up of lemmings, rodents, birds, fish, and some plants. They prefer lemmings, but will eat whatever is available.

Arctic foxes sometimes follow

polar bears to eat their leftovers.

Arctic foxes have very good hearing. They listen for sounds of movement under the snow.

When they hear something move, they pounce and punch through the ice with their paws to catch their prey.

Red foxes also pounce into

the snow to catch their prey.

Communication

Arctic foxes are usually quiet, but they do make some sounds to communicate.

When Arctic foxes are in danger, they make a high-pitched cry. They can also make a yowling sound.

Many sounds made by Arctic foxes are between parents and their babies.

Movement

Arctic foxes have been known to run at speeds of up to thirty miles per hour. This is usually for short distances. They don't run that fast for very long.

They sometimes slip and skid on the ice when running.

Arctic foxes will run from

predators such as wolves or

polar bears.

Coloration

Arctic foxes have white fur for most of the year. It changes to brown and gray in the summer, when there is less snow.

This helps them to blend in with their surroundings.

The color of their fur helps them

when they are hunting. They can

sneak up on prey.

Arctic Fox Life

Arctic foxes are **solitary** for most of the year. This means that they usually live alone.

They live in burrows that they dig deep into the snow. Their burrows help them to stay warm in the cold winter weather.

Arctic fox dens usually have

more than one entrance. They

are full of tunnels.

Arctic Fox Kits

Arctic foxes have a litter of between six and eight babies. They are called pups or kits.

Kits are usually born in the summer. They are ready to leave their parents by their first winter.

Both the mother and father

help to take care of the kits

when they are young.

Lifespan

Arctic foxes usually live between three and six years in the wild. They may live as long as fourteen years in **captivity**.

Their **lifespan** in the wild often depends on how much food is available.

Arctic foxes may live longer

when more food is available.

Population

In most areas, Arctic fox populations are **stable**. There are a few islands in the Bering Sea where they are very low.

Populations of Arctic foxes change based on how much food is available to them.

Arctic foxes are facing threats

like hunting, disease, and

habitat loss.

Helping Arctic Foxes

Arctic foxes are sometimes hunted for their fur. They are also hunted by people who believe they are pests.

In many places, people who hunt Arctic foxes must have a special license. This makes sure that they are not **overhunted**.

Temperatures in the Arctic have been getting warmer. This is causing ice to melt, which is not good for Arctic foxes.

There are groups that are helping Arctic foxes. They want to try to stop the change in temperature so that habitats are not destroyed.

Glossary

Adaptations: changes over time that help an animal survive

Captivity: animals that are kept by humans, not in the wild

Coast: where the land meets the ocean

Lifespan: how long an animal is expected to live

Omnivore: an animal that eats plants and animals

Overhunted: when too many of an animal are hunted

Predator: an animal that hunts other animals

Solitary: living alone

Stable: steady, unchanging

Victoria Blakemore is a first grade

teacher in Southwest Florida with a

passion for reading.

You can visit her at

www.elementaryexplorers.com

Also in This Series

Also in This Series